FREDERICK HOYOS
JORGE GÓMEZ
VELSSY HERNÁNDEZ

SDN IMPLEMENTATION USING FLOODLIGHT CONTROLLER

FREDERICK HOYOS
JORGE GÓMEZ
VELSSY HERNÁNDEZ

SDN IMPLEMENTATION USING FLOODLIGHT CONTROLLER

Configuring networks with Floodlight

ScienciaScripts

Imprint

Cover image: www.ingimage.com

This book is a translation from the original published under ISBN 978-613-9-40481-0.

Publisher:
Sciencia Scripts
is a trademark of
Dodo Books Indian Ocean Ltd. and OmniScriptum S.R.L publishing group

120 High Road, East Finchley, London, N2 9ED, United Kingdom
Str. Armeneasca 28/1, office 1, Chisinau MD-2012, Republic of Moldova, Europe
Printed at: see last page
ISBN: 978-620-8-08416-5

ABOUT THE AUTHORS:

FREDERICK HOYOS FRANCO
He is a systems engineer, graduated from the University of Córdoba. Full stack programmer. Knowledge in SQL, MySQL, PostgreSQL, VSCode, Microsoft SQL Server - Intermediate. Programming Languages: Java (Basic), Matlab, Python (Intermediate) ReactJS (Basic).

JORGE GOMEZ GOMEZ
Systems Engineer by profession graduated from Fundación Universitaria San Martín, Master in Telematics Engineering from Universidad del Cauca, PhD in Information Technology and Communications from the University of Granada Spain, full time professor of Systems Engineering at the University of Cordoba. Director of the SOCRATES research group of the Systems Engineering program at the University of Cordoba, Editor-in-Chief of the Engineering and Innovation magazine of the University of Cordoba. Member and founder of the IEEE student branch of the University of Cordoba. I have published numerous articles in the area of Internet of Things, Context Awareness, e-learning, telecommunications networks, in different journals indexed in JCR and SCOPUS indexes. I have developed research projects related to citizen security, smart cities, Internet of Things for health issues, among others. I am the coordinator of the Pervasive Computing research group of the Systems Engineering program at the University of Córdoba. In this research group we develop research activities oriented to intelligent systems based on technologies such as RFID, NFC, QRCODE, geolocation systems, ubiquitous and pervasive systems. Also in this seedbed students propose solutions in the above mentioned topics; members actively participate inside and outside the university in research activities. As a result, many members have won regional and national awards. In addition, I have participated as a jury evaluator of indexed journals, master's and doctoral theses. I am also guest editor of the journal Computational and Mathematical Methods in Medicine-Hindawi. I have been invited professor at the Corporación Universitaria de la Costa, in the doctorate of Information and Communication Technologies, in the subject Semantic Representation of Information in Ubiquitous Environments. I have been a professor at the Universidad Cooperativa de Colombia in Monteria from 2008 to 2015, where I taught courses in artificial intelligence, databases and telecommunications networks. Similarly, I was a professor at the Universidad del Sinú from 2008 to 2015, where I was also director of the GNOCIX research group of the Systems Engineering career. I have been a speaker at national and international events. At the international level I was invited by the State Technical University of Quevedo Ecuador to give a seminar on Internet of Things in 2014. In 2016 I was invited by the University of Babahoyo Ecuador to give a workshop seminar on Ubiquitous Systems. I have participated in internal calls for research at the University of Cordoba, as well as in external calls such as Minciencias.
Finally I can say that with the experience I have had over the years as a professional, I have contributed to generate new knowledge, this has been reflected in the articles I have published, the graduate work I have directed, the courses I have taught and the

appropriation of knowledge to the educational community. Within the IEEE Branch of the University of Cordoba, I have promoted research and social projection of knowledge to social environments that have required it.

Velssy Hernández Riaño:

She is a Systems Engineer and holds a Master's degree in Telematics Engineering from Universidad Francisco José de Caldas, Colombia. She is a Professor and Researcher of the SOCRATES research group of the Systems Engineering Department of the University of Córdoba.

Content

CHAPTER 1

THEORETICAL BACKGROUND.

Traditional networks are the old conventional way used to make network connections. These depend on specific network devices such as routers and switches to perform these network tasks, in order to control the traffic of these same networks; with modernization, the rise of technology companies and the scaling of these companies has created a concern regarding the issue of continuing to use this type of networks, because the performance is not appropriate as they grow, this is because the biggest problem of these networks is their difficult administration.

In these networks, all devices control themselves, so making any kind of change in order to update, upgrade or fix, involves a large investment of time, since each device must be configured manually, which increases the complexity and error.

The software-defined networking (SDN) paradigm has emerged in recent years as a new network architecture that enables flexible management of large-scale, highly complex networks. As noted by (Jiang et al., 2022) "SDN is a novel approach to designing, building, and managing networks that decouples the control plane and the forwarding plane."

The central idea behind SDN is to separate the network control plane (control plane) from the forwarding plane (data plane). As they explain (Jiang et al., 2022), "The premise of SDN is simple: decouple the forwarding plane from the control plane so that the packet forwarding (data plane) can be managed independently from a centralized SDN controller." This separation allows the "intelligence" of the network to be concentrated in the SDN controller, which has a centralized view of the entire network. Forwarding devices become simpler, focusing only on forwarding packets according to rules imposed by the central controller.

One of the key enablers of this architecture is that "network devices are programmable through well-defined interfaces between the control plane and the forwarding plane" (Alotaibi et al., 2022). That is, the SDN controller can program the behavior of network switches and routers in a flexible manner.

That is why SDN thus seeks to provide administrators with centralized tools to program, virtualize and monitor in real time, enabling the adaptability of networks. The promise includes accelerating the evolution of data centers to a more advanced generation with greater scalability, automation and task simplification. In SDN, packet processing does not rely on static configurations, but is based on a dynamic structure through a software layer, decoupling it from the physical infrastructure.

SDN promises to make networks more agile and easier to manage by centralizing control, decoupling the forwarding plane from the control plane, and making network devices programmable. This emerging architecture is gaining adoption in data centers, service providers, and enterprises.

SDN definition.

SDN has had a revolutionary approach to the design and management of computer networks, which has allowed it to be encompassed in several points:

First. Input Feature Representation.

In the representation of input characteristics, a centralized controller, as the key component, interacts with distributed network devices and applications. All these inputs are network topology or device state, which are represented in a structured way in order to allow dynamic and centralized control of the same (Jimenez et al., 2021).

Second. Classification Function.

This classification function in SDN is achieved through a central controller that computes and manages all decisions in a network. This controller is often based on standards such as OpenFlow, which enables dynamic and centralized decision making for functions such as routing, resource allocation, and policy management (Wazirali et al., 2021).

Third. Objective Function for Learning.

SDNs seek to optimize the performance and utilization of network resources in order to reduce dependence on manual configuration or constant human labor intervention, allowing rapid adaptation to changes in traffic demand or network topology (Pei et al., 2020).

Fourth. Algorithm to Optimize the Objective function.

SDNs implement different types of algorithms and protocols, one of which we have mentioned above is OpenFlow, which seeks to optimize the objective function. These algorithms enable communication between the SDN controller and the network devices, which facilitates decision making in a centralized and dynamic way (Das and Gurusamy, 2021)).

Fifth. BDS Phases.

SDN is divided into multiple phases, each of which has its own purpose and means of adaptation, which is essential to maintain optimal performance in changing environments.

Sixth. Practical Applications.

These are diverse in SDN, as they range from efficient resource management and rapid service deployment to adaptability to network changes.

Seventh. Aspects of Testing and Evaluation.

This involves measuring metrics such as latency, bandwidth utilization and resource efficiency. These tests ensure that SDN meets network improvement objectives and adapts effectively to different scenarios.

Network architecture.

The architecture of a conventional data network is based on the distinction between two essential logical components: the infrastructure plane, the data plane and the control plane. These elements work together to ensure connectivity and the effective flow of data within the network, playing specific roles that are crucial to its efficient operation and optimal management.

Infrastructure Plan.

This plane consists of the physical network devices, such as routers, switches and other network equipment. These devices form the infrastructure over which SDN is implemented. In the context of SDN architecture, the infrastructure plane is responsible for transmitting data packets according to the instructions provided by the control plane.

Data Plane.

The data plane is responsible for the transfer of data packets across the network. This component is composed of intermediate devices such as routers, switches and other network elements, all of which are generated by users and other headers aggregated by the layers of the OSI model that transit a given network.

Their main function is to route and forward data packets efficiently from their origin to their destination, following previously defined routing rules. On the data plane, the intermediate devices operate autonomously and without external intervention to ensure connectivity and data flow in the network.

Control Plane.

The control plane is the brain of the network, responsible for managing and coordinating the operations of intermediate devices in the data plane. In contrast to the data plane, the control plane centralizes the intelligence of the network in a component known as the controller. The controller is responsible for making routing and traffic management decisions on the network, as well as dynamically adapting to changing network conditions. Using communication protocols such as OpenFlow, the controller interacts with intermediate devices to program their behavior and ensure consistent network operation.

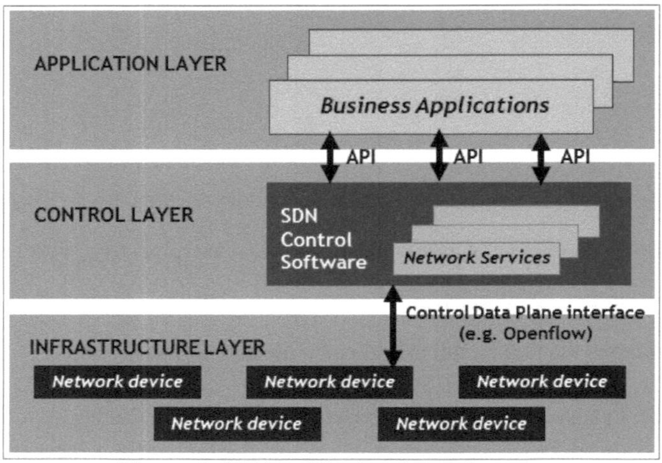

Figure 1. *SDN architecture taken from (https://www.sdxcentral.com/networking/sdn/definitions/what-the-definition-of-software-defined-networking-sdn/)*

Figure 1 shows in a logical way how the SDN architecture works. It can be seen how the network is centralized in software-based SDN controllers. This centralization allows enterprises and communications service providers to gain independence and control over their entire network infrastructure from a single logical point, leading to significant simplification in network design and operation.

The centralized approach of SDN also has a major impact on the simplification of network devices. Unlike devices in conventional network architectures, which are often burdened with the task of processing numerous standard protocols, devices in an SDN network must simply accept instructions from SDN controllers. This allows them to focus on packet forwarding tasks without the additional burden of processing and managing high-level protocols, resulting in more efficient and simplified devices.

SDN emulation tools.

SDN tools are those that allow us to configure a simulation environment or emulation of networks within the same system, which allows us to set up a network scenario using "Topologies" and "Traffic Flows", all this managed from a single computer thanks to these tools, also allow modification or changes without having to stop the services, which is useful to check how these changes affect the system.

Among the SDN tools, we have the following:

1. Mininet: Enables the creation of customized network topologies and the emulation of SDN networks.
2. GNS3: Incorporates support for SDN and is versatile for network simulation.
3. Cisco Packet Tracer: One of the best known in the SDN field, providing a platform for simulation and experimentation.
4. NS-3: Provides a flexible and extensible environment for studying network behavior.
5. Colibri: Allows studies on the different tools for architecture emulation and simulation.
6. Open Network Emulator: Provides a platform that enables the creation of complex virtual networks and supports SDN emulation.
7. CORE: Allows the construction of complex topologies.

8. EstiNet: Focuses on accurate emulation of network behaviors and provides a platform for testing and validating SDN applications and controllers.
9. OMNeT++: Provides a platform for developing and testing network algorithms and protocols.

Several of these tools are somewhat known, while others are not or have very little information on how they work, but were added for the sake of knowledge.

OpenFlow protocol.

The OpenFlow protocol is fundamental in the context of software-defined networking (SDN), enabling centralized and programmable network management. Originally developed to operate over Ethernet switches, it has become an open standard for communication between an SDN controller and switching devices.

The OpenFlow standard was conceived at Stanford University in response to the growing need for innovation in networks, which had become a critical infrastructure. It was observed that innovation in the network was increasingly hampered, which led to the proposal of network virtualization, dividing it into a production and an experimental part. It was in this direction that the OpenFlow project, which is still under development, was launched.

The OpenFlow protocol is based on three fundamental pillars:

- **Programmability:** Facilitates network management by allowing administrators to program networks according to specific needs.
- **Centralized intelligence:** Enables better performance based on distributed management policies and simple provisioning by centralizing network intelligence.

- **Abstraction:** Evident in the separation of software and hardware, resulting in the decoupling of the control plane and data plane.

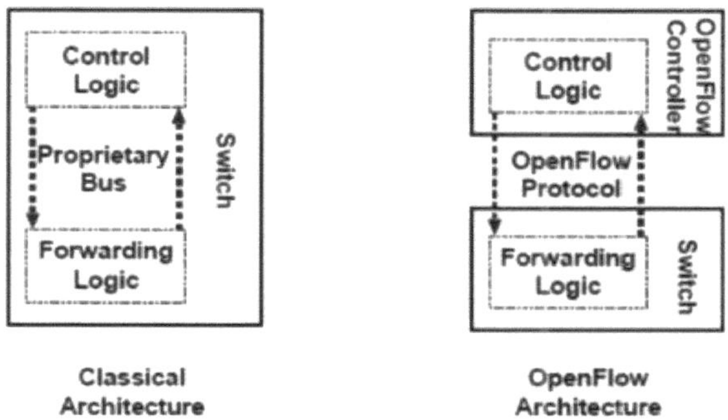

Figure 2. *OpenFlow architecture taken from (Waziraıi et al., 2021).*

In a classic router or switch, traffic management (data plane) and high-level routing decisions (control plane) occur on the same device. In contrast, an Open vSwitch or OpenFlow Switch separates these two functions. The data plane tasks reside on the switch, while the high-level routing decisions move to an isolated controller, usually a standard server. Communication between the Open vSwitch and the controller is done through the OpenFlow protocol.

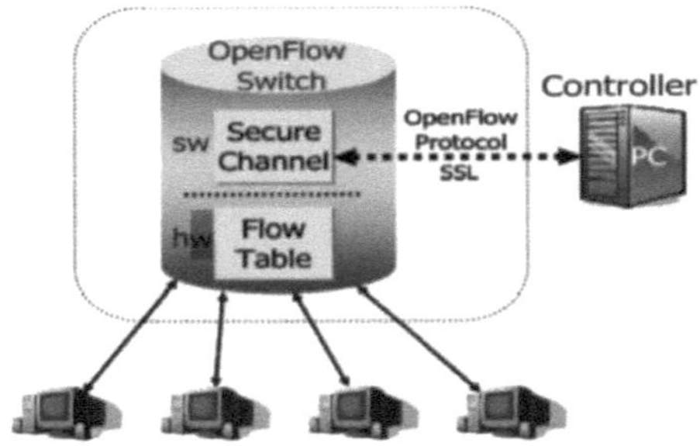

Figure 3. *OpenvSwitch architecture taken from (https://openzen.wordpress.com/2015/02/23/protocolo-openflow/).*

The Open vSwitch presents a clean flow table abstraction, where each entry contains a set of packet fields according to the topology and a corresponding action. When an OpenFlow switch receives a packet for which it has no matching flow entries, it forwards it to the controller for a handling decision. This enables a granular SDN architecture that is responsive to real-time changes from applications or users.

OpenFlow is being implemented as a feature in commercial Ethernet switches, routers and wireless access points, providing a standard to enable research experiments without the need to expose the internal workings of network devices. Major network device vendors are enabling this protocol in commercially available switches.

The implementation of OpenFlow as a feature in commercial network devices has allowed researchers to conduct experiments and tests without relying on vendors to access the inner workings of network devices. This has facilitated innovation and development in the networking field, while fostering collaboration and knowledge sharing in the scientific and network engineering community.

The adoption of OpenFlow by leading network device vendors signals a significant shift in the network design and management paradigm. By enabling OpenFlow in commercially available switches, these vendors are giving users the ability to deploy and manage networks more flexibly and efficiently, better adapting to the changing needs of applications and users.

Mininet

Mininet is an emulator that allows you to create networks of virtual machines, switches, controllers and links, implemented on a physical device running the standard Linux kernel. It stands out for its ability to simulate highly flexible custom routing and other peculiarities of software-defined networking (SDN), thanks to its support for OpenFlow on switches.

In addition to its usefulness in research, development, learning and prototyping, Mininet provides an economical and efficient environment for testing, debugging and other network-related tasks. Its command-line interface (CLI) simplifies network configuration and control, making it easy for multiple developers to work on the same topology.

Mininet's flexibility extends to the ability to create complex topologies without the need for physical hardware, as well as its Python API that enables creation and experimentation with custom networks. This versatility makes Mininet a valuable tool for both design validation and performance evaluation of SDN systems.

It is important to keep in mind the limitations of Mininet, such as the restriction of bandwidth and processing power of the assigned server, as well as the dependency on Linux-compatible applications. However, its ability to run real code on emulated networks makes it easy to transition designs developed in Mininet to production environments with minimal changes.

In addition to providing a virtual environment and testbed for SDN, Mininet enables collaboration of multiple developers on the same topology and offers a detailed view of system behavior by emulating real networks.

its ability to simulate complex networks and run real code, Mininet offers several features that distinguish it as an invaluable tool for development and experimentation in the field of software-defined networking (SDN):

- **Cost-effective test environment:** Mininet provides a cost-effective test environment by enabling the creation of virtual networks on a standard physical device running the Linux kernel. This eliminates the need for expensive and complicated hardware, making SDN experimentation more accessible to a wide range of users, from students to industry professionals.
- **Flexibility in topology creation:** With Mininet, complex network topologies can be easily created and modified without the need to wire a physical network. This allows users to design and test a variety of network configurations to suit different scenarios and application requirements.
- **Support for multiple developers:** Mininet allows multiple developers to work concurrently and independently on the same network topology. This facilitates collaboration on SDN projects and fosters an agile and collaborative development environment.
- **Extensible Python API:** Mininet's Python API makes it easy to create and experiment with custom networks. Users can use this API to automate tasks, develop new functionality and perform extensive testing on their SDN applications.
- **Smooth transition to real hardware:** Thanks to its ability to run real code and emulate the behavior of physical networks, Mininet enables a seamless

transition from development and testing in emulated environments to deployment on real hardware. This helps reduce the time and costs associated with deploying SDN solutions in production environments.

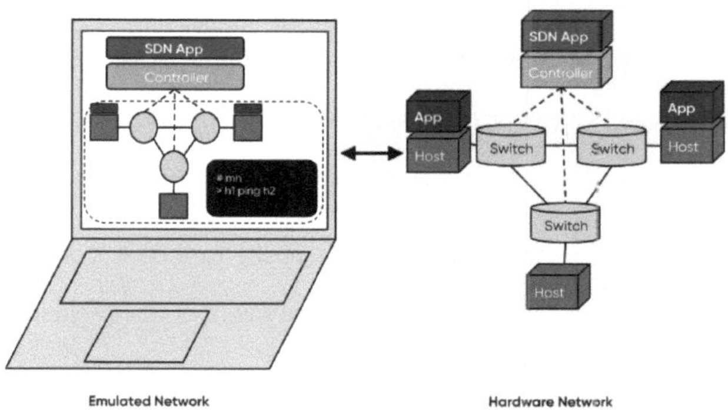

Figure 4. *Mininet architecture taken from (https://incyt.upse.edu.ec/ciencia/revistas/index.php/rctu/article/view/489/555)*

CHAPTER 2.

Virtual Machines

One of the tools that has contributed most to the use of SDNs are virtual machines. To say that they are fundamental pillars for its continued development is no exaggeration. Thanks to them, anyone can implement SDN without putting their equipment at risk due to an incorrect configuration, in addition to the possibility of using multiple machines that allow the implementation of several SDNs simultaneously.

Its operation is not very complicated, and its ability to create isolated and flexible environments is of great help in the efficient deployment of SDN solutions.

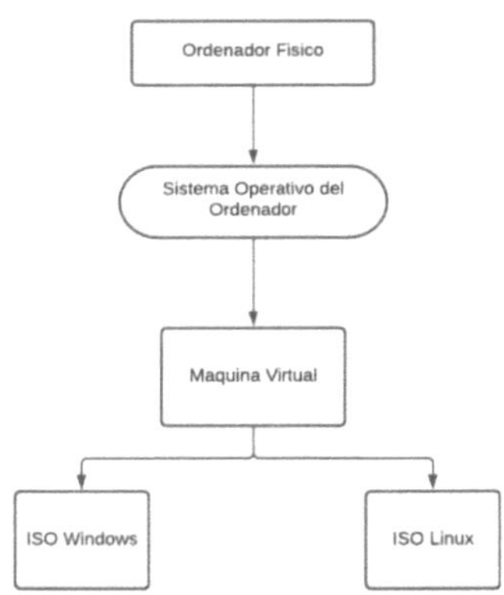

Figure 5. *SDN infrastructure*

As we can see in Figure 5, creating an infrastructure to work with is not very complicated in a virtual machine, as long as we have the necessary parts to make use of the tool, which allows us to manage it according to our needs.

Foundation

Within the field of computing, the first signs of publications on the field of virtual machines are reflected for the first time in 1944, practically at a time when computer science was not in vogue. It is a year in which there is an academic publication that is not directly related to computer science, but under an analysis and interpretation ignites the idea of the first signs of the use and relationship of the two words together of virtual machine. Under the use of bibliometrics in the Scopus database by the author Berresford, A et al (1944) in which he comes to speak of a pollen extracting machine, the document comes to mention the words virtual machine, but the use of the word virtual comes to have a definition that has evolved over the years. At that time it was focused on the conceptual representation of situations and strategic decisions in which the closest interpretation was about a "Simulation", strategies and decisions that were not based on real events or conditions; but on theoretical or imaginary situations; being this the argument of direct relation in the evolution of the virtua word more specifically "The virtual machine", having as relation a specific term which is simulation because the simulation implies to imitate or represent a system or process, often in a controlled environment, to understand its behavior, to test hypothesis or in training.

The term "virtual machine" has its historical origins in the 1960s, when IBM began developing virtualization technology for its mainframes. According to Goldberg (1974), the virtual machine is "an efficient and isolated duplication of the physical machine using shared hardware resources". A machine that separates the essence of the presence of hardware that allows the creation of a computing environment that emulates and behaves as if it were a real computer (physical machine), but without the need to have the physical hardware dedicated only to it. In essence, a virtual machine is a software environment that emulates a real computer and can run programs as if it were a separate physical computer (Jiang and Zhou, 2013). Virtual machines provide abstraction from the underlying hardware and allow physical resources to be shared among several virtual environments isolated from each other (Wang et al., 2008).

As Crosby (2007) explains, virtualization involves "the decoupling of a service resource from the physical dependency that constrains it". In this sense, virtual machines decouple the actual hardware from the operating systems and applications, thus enabling the consolidation of multiple workloads on less hardware. The virtual machine is an epistemological concept that denotes an isolated and portable software environment that simulates a real computer system, allowing multiple programs and operating systems to run on the same physical infrastructure.

Virtual Machine Consolidation

Over the years, it has become evident how the fundamental role of virtual machines has gradually and skillfully emerged, bringing a crucial dimension to flexibility and efficiency. Now, it is the need to represent how this fantastic tool converges with SDN and enhances its dynamic ecosystem.

Within the SDN world, virtual machines do not simply refer to environments that are isolated, but to strategic elements that enhance the agility and adaptability of networks; that is, they are extended to act as live actors in the scheduling and orchestration of resources, functioning as a catalyst in the execution of services and aligning with the dynamic demands of the environment, to a certain extent.

However, within this consonance there are key elements for the functioning of this integration, which are:

- Control Centralization: The centralization of control in SDNs finds its natural complement in the ability of virtual machines to operate in isolated environments and respond to centralized commands, creating a symphony of dynamic management and efficient scheduling.
- Extended Programmability: Programmability, the cornerstone of SDNs, extends to virtual machines, triggering real-time adaptability and facilitating instantaneous changes in the network.

We can also find applications that are synthesized in depth, such as:

- Agile Service Deployment: Virtual machine integration enables agile deployment of services in SDNs, from rapid deployment of new functions to instant adaptation to changing network requirements.
- Resource Optimization: By consolidating resources through the use of virtual machines we can perceive an operational efficiency and also a means that serves as a catalyst in the integral optimization of the network in the context of SDN.
- Resiliency and Recovery: By acting as flexible and replicable entities, virtual machines strengthen the resiliency of SDN, giving us multiple robust options for failover and service continuity.

Virtual machines make it possible to quickly deploy new network services in isolated environments over the SDN infrastructure. For example, a virtual machine with a firewall can be deployed in minutes without affecting other parts of the network. The SDN controller can then orchestrate and replicate this firewall service to other areas of the network in a flexible manner as needed.

Taking into account all these functionalities and utilities that virtual machines are capable of providing, it can be deduced that it is a sufficiently apt tool to explore the continuous world of possibilities that exist within SDN. This union of virtual machines and SDN will give us an effective implementation and efficient management of modern networks.

Use of the Virtual Machine.

Virtual machines (VMs) allow the execution of multiple operating systems and applications on a single physical server. Each VM has its own virtualized components such as CPU, RAM, storage and network nic (Diaz et al., 2021). The hypervisor or virtualization software creates and manages these VMs, dynamically allocating resources and isolating them from each other.

On the other hand, software-defined networking (SDN) separates the network control plane from the data forwarding plane (Yang and Yeung, 2020). The control plane is centralized in a programmable SDN controller. The forwarding plane uses standard network devices, but they become managed and programmable through the controller.

VMs and SDN complement each other to provide flexible and scalable data center infrastructures. The hypervisor can create isolated virtual networks to interconnect VMs, while the SDN controller provides network connectivity and management between physical hosts (Yoo et al., 2022). Together, they enable the consolidation of many virtualized workloads onto less physical hardware.

Specifically, VMs leverage SDN capabilities in the following ways:

Centralized management and global visibility: The SDN controller has a unified view of the physical and virtual topology, simplifying operations such as monitoring, provisioning and troubleshooting (Aryan et al., 2022).

- Simplified migration: Network policies and configurations can migrate along with VMs as they move between hosts, without the need for manual reconfiguration (Qu, 2020).
- Dynamic virtual networks: SDN controllers can create and manage virtual overlay networks to connect VMs in a flexible and agile way (Umar et al., 2021).
- Segmentation and isolation: VM traffic can be separated into distinct virtual network segments for greater security and isolation.
- Load balancing: The SDN controller has visibility of traffic between VMs and can distribute it to optimize performance (Hamdan et al , 2021).

Virtualization and SDN complement each other powerfully. VMs provide consolidation and isolation while SDN delivers centralized management, programmability and flexible connectivity between virtualized environments. This interrelationship has driven their joint adoption in data centers and clouds.

CHAPTER 3

FLOODLIGHT

Floodlight is an open source platform based on software-defined networking (SDN) that acts as a centralized controller for network management and configuration. This controller was developed by an open community of developers, many of whom belong to Big Switch Networks, which uses the OpenFlow protocol to orchestrate traffic flows in a software-defined networking (SDN) environment.

Floodlight is used to implement and manage software-defined networks, which separate the control plane from the data plane in a network, allowing greater flexibility, scalability and control over the network infrastructure.

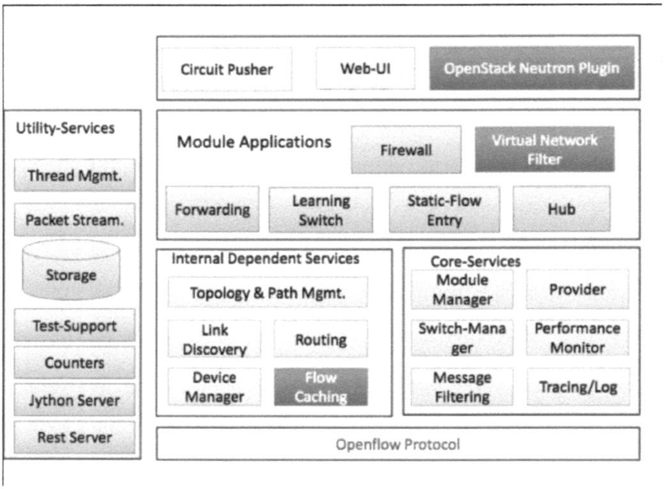

Figure 6. *Floodlight architecture taken from (https://www.researchgate.net/figure/Floodlight-Architecture_fig1_345322626)*

The SDN controller is responsible for maintaining all network rules and providing the necessary instructions to the underlying infrastructure on how traffic should be handled. This allows enterprises to better adapt to their changing needs and have better control over their networks.

Floodlight features.

1. **Open Source:** Floodlight is an open source SDN controller, which means that its source code is publicly available for inspection, modification and contribution by the community.
2. **Java-based:** Floodlight is written in Java, making it cross-platform and compatible with a wide range of operating systems.
3. **RESTful interface:** Provides a RESTful application programming interface (API) that allows developers and administrators to interact with the controller programmatically, facilitating automation and integration with other tools and systems.
4. **Support for SDN protocols**: Floodlight supports several SDN protocols, such as OpenFlow, which enables communication between the controller and compatible network switches.
5. **Scalability:** It is designed to be scalable and can handle networks of different sizes, from lab environments to large-scale enterprise deployments.
6. **Modularity:** Floodlight is designed with a modular architecture that allows for easy extension and customization by adding new modules and functionalities.
7. **Active community:** As an open source project, Floodlight has an active community of developers and users who contribute improvements, bug fixes and new features.

Services Model.

Floodlight follows a service model based on modules that provide different functionalities and capabilities. These modules can be enabled or disabled according to the specific needs of the network. The following are some of the main modules and services available in Floodlight:

- **Core Controller**

  It is the core Floodlight module that manages the logic and core functions of the SDN controller. It provides basic services such as network topology discovery, routing, flow management and general controller administration.

- **Flow Management Service (Flow Management Service)**

  This service is responsible for the management and control of data flows in the network. It allows the definition of routing rules, quality of service (QoS) policies and traffic congestion management.

- **Topology Discovery Service (Topology Discovery Service)**

  This service is responsible for discovering and maintaining up-to-date network topology information. It provides information about the connected network devices, the links between them and the overall network structure.

- **Security Service**

  This service deals with network security and threat protection. It can include functions such as intrusion detection and prevention, firewall and network access control.

- **Virtualization Service**

  This service allows the creation and management of virtual networks within the physical network infrastructure. It allows resource sharing, network isolation and segmentation, and the creation of virtualized network environments.

- **Monitoring and Analytics Service**

  This service is responsible for collecting data and statistics on network performance, traffic and other relevant parameters. It provides real-time monitoring tools and data analysis to assist in network optimization and troubleshooting.

Components.

Floodlight, as an open source SDN controller, is composed of several key components that work together to provide network management and configuration functionalities. The main components of Floodlight are described below:

- **Core Controller**

  It is the core component of Floodlight that handles the logic and core functionalities of the SDN controller. It is responsible for receiving and processing messages from network devices, as well as making routing and flow control decisions.

- **Modules**

  Floodlight is designed with a modular architecture that allows the incorporation of different modules according to specific needs. These modules can provide additional functionalities, such as policy management, security, virtualization, monitoring, among others. Some examples of common modules include the Flow Manager module, Topology Manager module, Security Manager module, etc.

- **API (Application Programming Interface)**

  Floodlight provides an API that allows developers and network administrators to interact with the controller. The API allows programming and control of Floodlight's functionality, which facilitates integration with other applications and tools.

- **OpenFlow Protocol**

  Floodlight communicates with network devices through the OpenFlow protocol, which is a standard protocol used in software-defined networking (SDN). The OpenFlow protocol allows the controller to interact with compatible switches and routers to control data flow and make routing decisions.

- **Administration interface**

  Floodlight offers a web-based administration interface that allows users to configure and manage the network. This interface provides access to different functionalities and tools for network configuration and monitoring.

CHAPTER 4.

INSTALLATION GUIDE.

Virtual Machine (Virtual Box).

The virtual machine is the most important thing, so it is good to define one that meets the necessary criteria to be able to work without inconveniences, in this case we will use one of the most recommended, which is VirtualBox, an application created by the

```
$ https://www.virtualbox.org/
```

Oracle company, which will help to emulate an independent machine on the computer. To install VirtualBox, it is necessary to download the installer from its page, which can be found below.

Once you click on the link, it will redirect you to the page, which will allow you to download the installer that goes according to your operating system, in this case the operating system you are using is **Windows 11**, so the installer you need to run the system is the Windows installer, which proceeds to download and will throw an installation file.

Download VM Floodlight image.

In order to work with Floodlight, it is necessary to have an operating system that fits the functionalities, services and dependencies that it can offer, but Floodlight, in turn, provides a virtual machine preconfigured with Mininet, Open vSwitch and Floodlight itself, which facilitates the installation and the saving of possible problems when configuring.

For this, it is necessary to go to the official Floodlight community page which can be

```
$ https://floodlight.atlassian.net/wiki/spaces
```

found at the following link:

Once you click on the link, it will redirect you to the page, in which you can find different sections, where you will access the one called "Floodlight Controller", here inside you will find everything related to the controller, including the normal installation, documentation, the Web GUI, among others. The necessary section will be "Floodlight VM", here you will find all the installation process provided by the community, as well as the option to download the preconfigured machine, which is the one you are going to use.

After this, a compressed folder in *".zip"* format will be downloaded, which will have to be unzipped to use the Floodlight *".vmdk"* file. Once the file is unzipped, open the *"VirtualBox"* program.

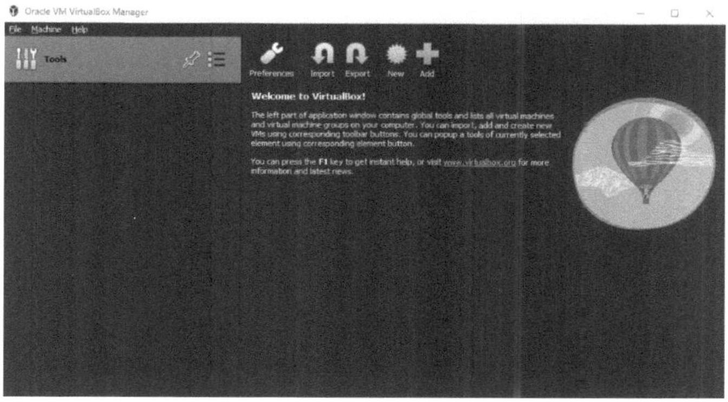

Figure 7. *VirtualBox environment*

After opening the *"VirtualBox"* program, look for the *"New"* button to create a virtual machine.

Figure 8. *VirtualBox Options Box*

Once you have found this option, click on it and it will open the following window:

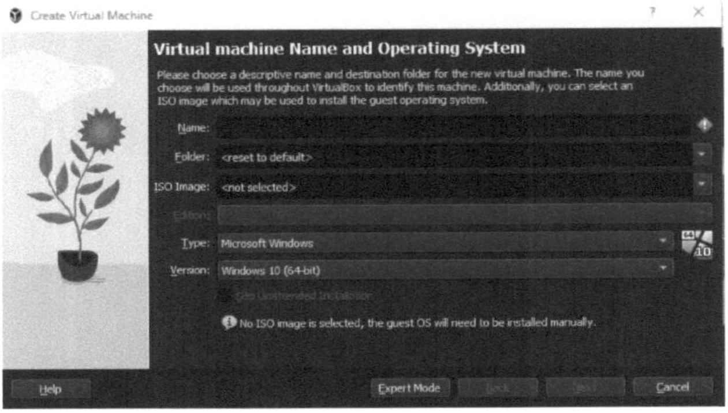

Figure 9. *Virtual Machine Creation*

Once inside, look for the *"Expert Mode"* button that appears at the bottom of the window and then click on it.

.

Figure 10. *Virtual Machine Creation (Expert Mode Option)*

Once clicked, it will show other sections of the previous section, which will look as follows:

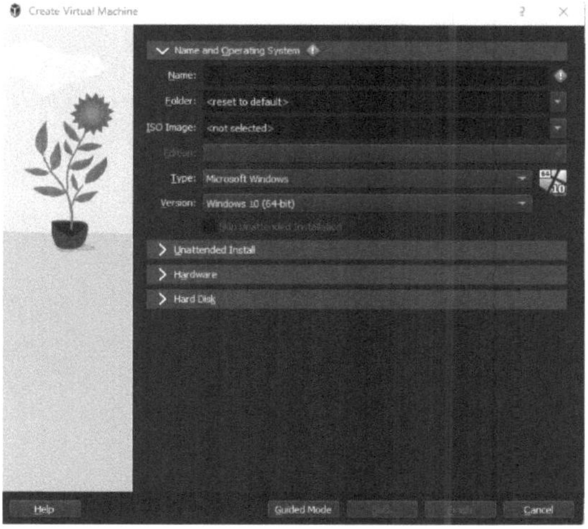

Figure 11. *Expert Mode VirtualBox*

After this, we proceed to add a name to the virtual machine, although we are going to use a preconfigured virtual machine, the process of implementation to the *"VirtualBox"*, for its later use, is as if we were creating a machine from scratch, since it is a *".vmdk"* file, which is being used and not a backup, as it is when it is an OVA.

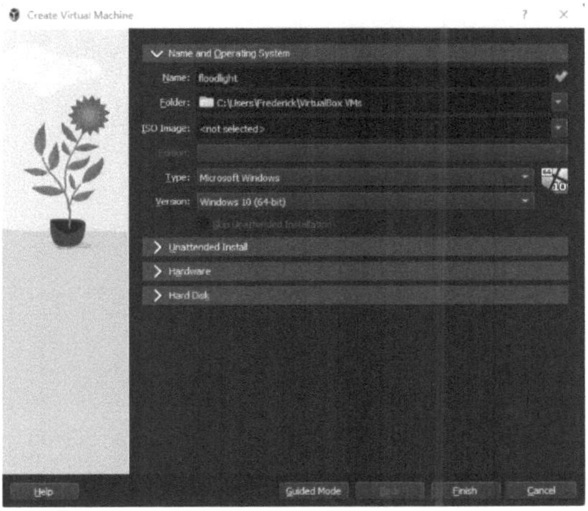

Figure 12. *Expert Mode VirtualBox (Name Selection)*

After this, we proceed to choose the type of system and the version, in this case we will use the type *"Linux"*, since we will use a system based on *"Linux"* and finally in the version we choose *"Ubuntu"*, as you can see.

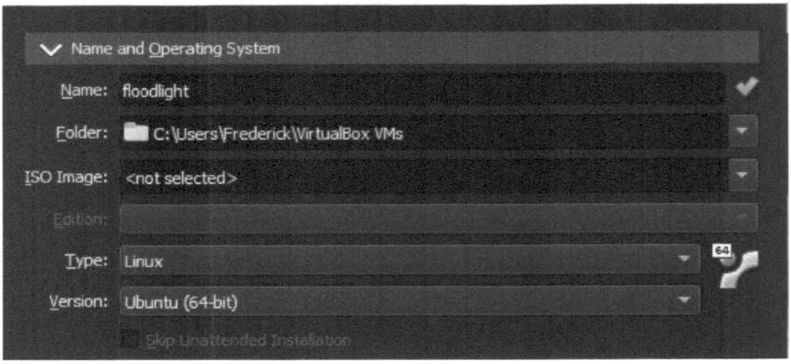

Figure 13. *Expert Mode VirtualBox (System Type Selection)*

Now, in the *"Hard Disk"* section, select the following option.

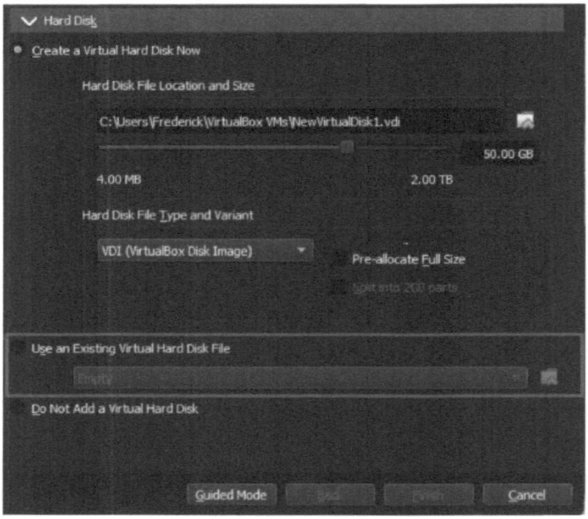

Figure 14. *Expert Mode VirtualBox (Hard Disk)*

Once the option is checked, proceed to click on the search button and then another window will open as shown below.

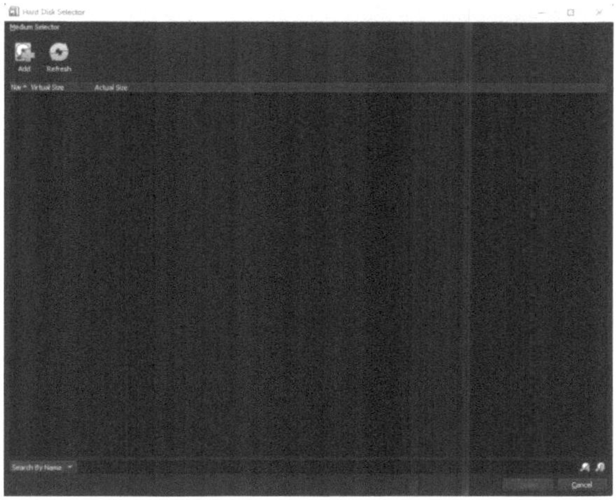

Figure 15. *Hard Disk Interface*

In this tab, click on the disk icon named *"Add"*.

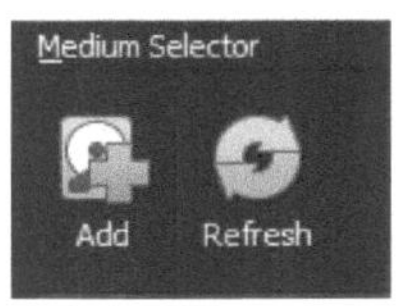

Figure 16. *Hard Disk Interface (Options Box)*

Now, once the button is clicked, a new window will be displayed where the Floodlight *".vmdk"* file must be searched and selected.

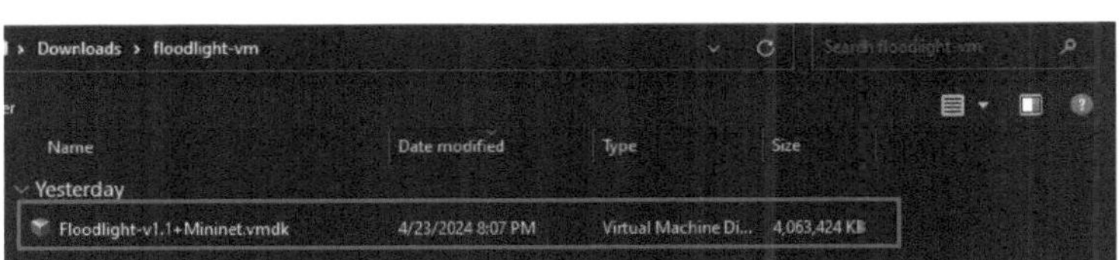

Figure 17. *Floodlight file*

Once selected, it will appear in the previously opened window as you can see below.

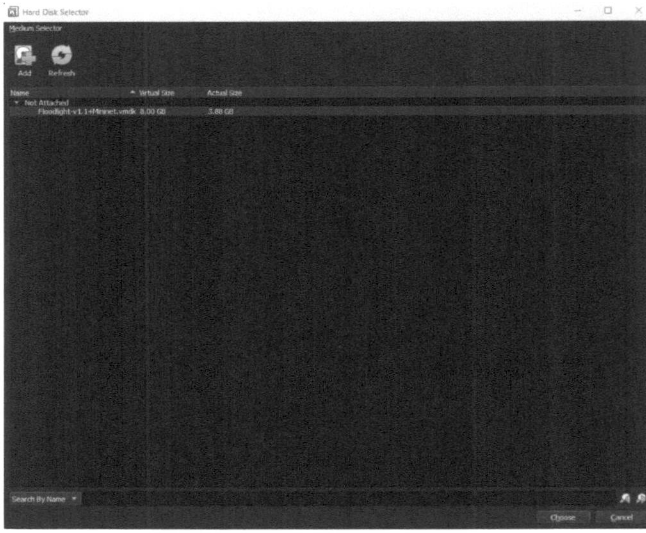

Figure 18. *Hard Disk Interface - Selection*

Here, click on *"Choose"* and it will remain selected in the disk section, as you can see.

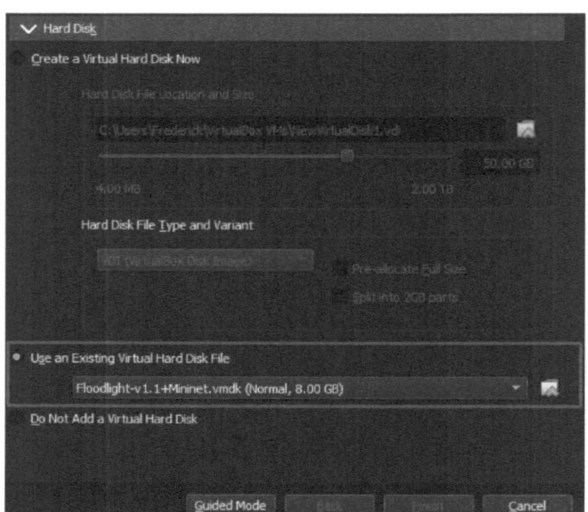

Figure 19. *VirtualBox Expert Mode (Hard Disk) #2*

Once all this is done, the configuration will be ready and proceed to click on the *"Finish"* button and this will immediately create the Floodlight virtual machine with all its preconfigurations as you can see.

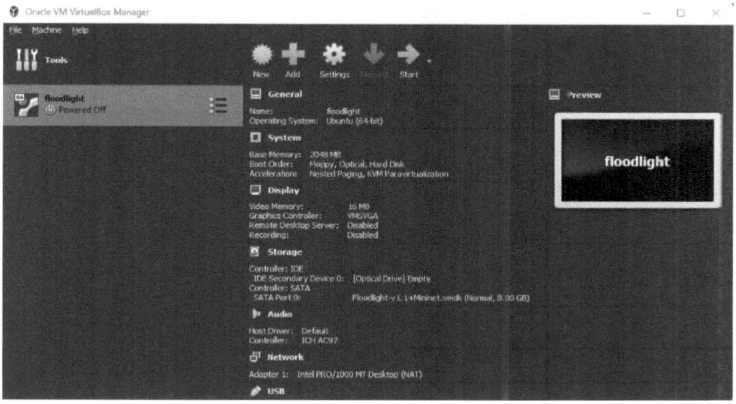

Figure 20. *VirtualBox environment - Floodlight*

Finally, the virtual machine is opened to check that everything is in optimal conditions and runs without any problem.

Figure 21. *Floodlight Virtual Machine*

As you can see, the Floodlight dedicated environment was executed in the best way, you may encounter a problem when opening as shown below.

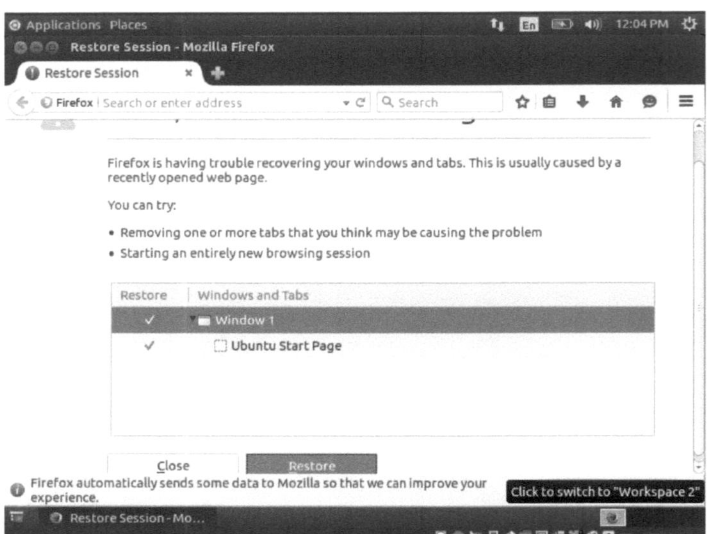

Figure 22. *Navigator - Floodlight environment*

This problem can simply be ignored as it is not relevant and does not affect the procedures ahead. The environment has a user and password defined by default, which is *"floodlight"*.

Preparation of the Environment.

To start preparing the environment, it is necessary to go to the Floodlight environment terminal or console, to do so, go to the *"Application"* section.

Figure 23. *Floodlight Virtual Machine (Applications)*

Now, it will be necessary to go to the main section of the virtual machine and it is necessary to *"right click"* on the virtual machine created previously and then go to the *"setting"* or *"configuration"* section.

Figure 24. *VirtualBox Environment (Machine Configuration)*

Then, you will see a section like the following one:

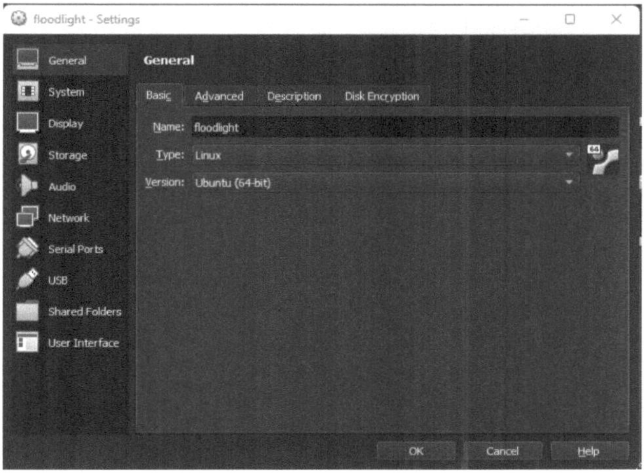

Figure 25. *Virtual Machine Configuration Environment*

Once inside, go to the *"network"* section as shown below:

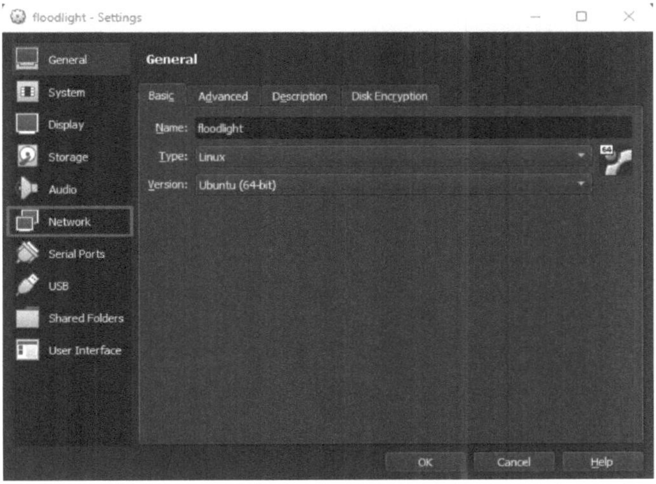

Figure 26. *Virtual Machine Configuration Environment (General)*

Once you are here, proceed to change the "NAT" connection for the "Bridged adapter" connection, once you have done that, you will see some options like the ones shown below:

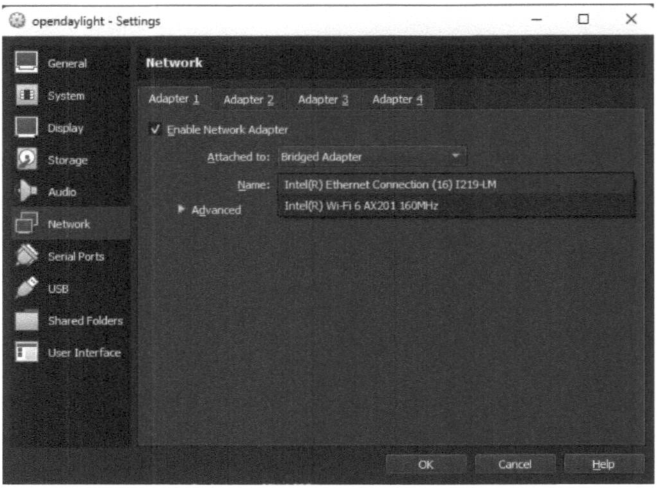

Figure 27. *Virtual Machine Configuration Environment (Network)*

These options will not be the same for everyone and may appear more than one, the important thing is that once the options are displayed it is important to know that the option *"Ethernet Connection"* or "Ethernet Connection" is for computers connected directly by cable to the router and the *"Wi-Fi Connection"* are for those that are connected wirelessly, it is important to choose the option based on this, after having explained this, we will proceed to choose the first option since the computer where you are currently working, is by direct connection.

After this is done, you will proceed to open the virtual machine again, in case you had the virtual machine open when you did this part, it is necessary to restart it.

Now, after all this has been done, it is necessary to go to the *"Application"* menu within the Floodlight environment and select the *"Accessories"* option and then *"Terminal"*.

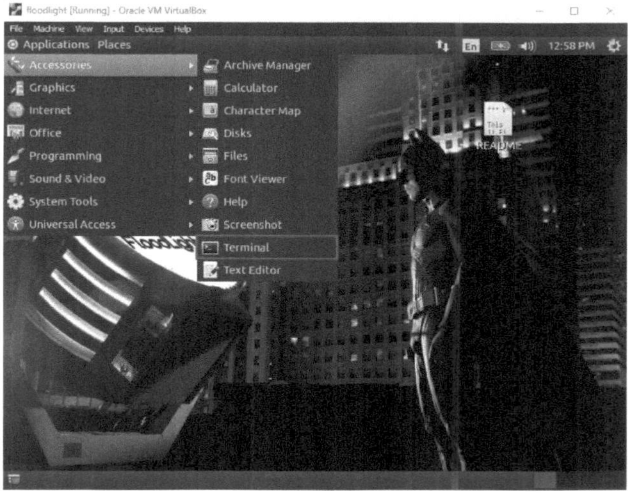

Figure 28. *Floodlight Options Box (Terminal)*

After that, it is necessary to type the following command:

```
$ ifconfig
```

This command is used to display information about the network interfaces on the system, this information can include IP addresses, MAC addresses, interface status and more.

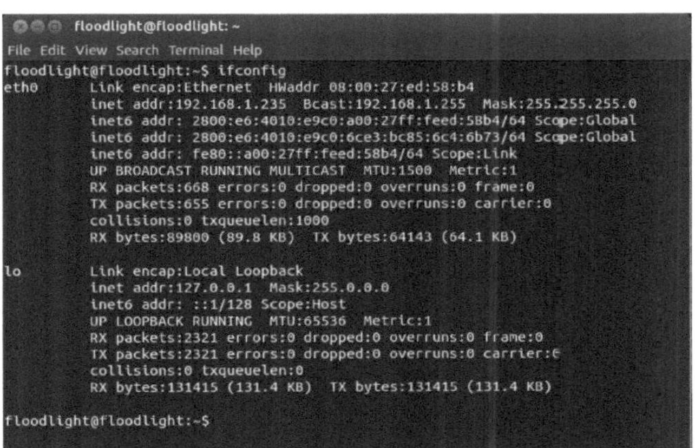

Figure 29. *Floodlight terminal (ifconfig)*

As you can see, you are shown the netmask section corresponding to the connection you are using, which may vary, in this case it is *"192.168.1.235"*.

Now, immediately the terminal will open, where you will type the following command:

```
$ cd floodlight
```

This command is used to change the current terminal directory to the directory in question, which is *"floodlight"*.

Figure 30. *Floodlight Terminal (Floodlight Folder)*

After typing the command and going to the *"floodlight"* folder, proceed to type the following command:

```
$ ant
```

This command is used to invoke the *"Apache Ant"* tool which is a build automation tool used in Java projects, such as Floodlight.

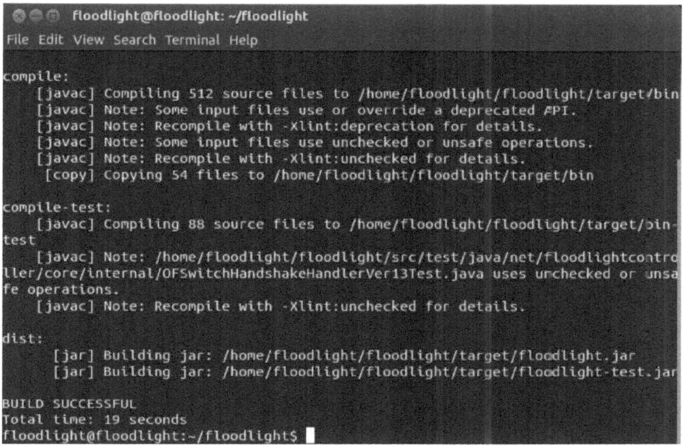

Figure 31. *Floodlight Terminal (Apache Ant)*

By executing this command, several tasks will be performed, such as compiling the source code, generating JAR files, performing tests, etc. These tasks depend on how the build.xml file is configured in the Floodlight project. You will know that it has finished executing when it returns *"BUILD SUCCESSFUL"* as shown in the figure.

Now proceed to type the following command:

```
$ java -jar target/floodlight.jar
```

This command is used to execute the JAR file generated after building the Floodlight project. This command starts the application and runs it in the Java Virtual Machine (JVM).

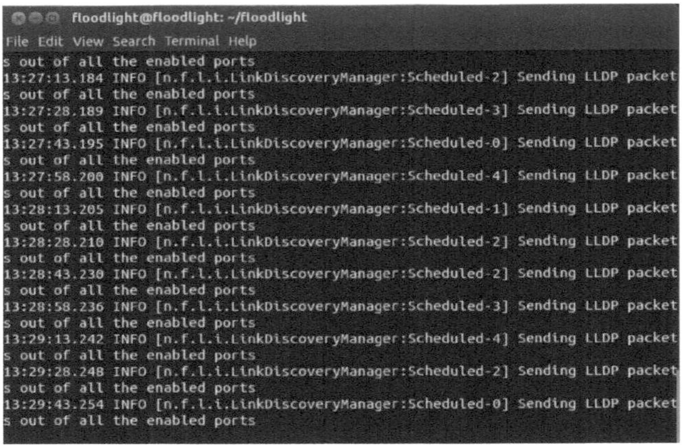

Figure 32. *Execution of JAR file*

After entering the command, it will remain running in the terminal you are using, then it is necessary to open a new terminal and once it is opened type the following command:

```
sudo apt install mininet
```

This command is used to install the Mininet tool that allows you to create virtual networks.

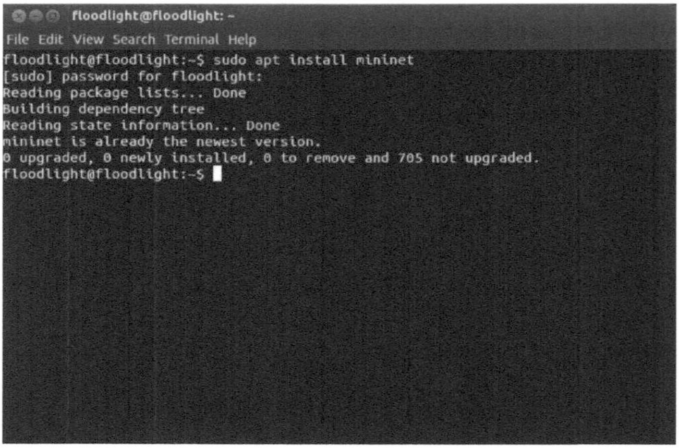

Figure 33. *Mininet installation*

Even though the preconfigured machine comes with *"Mininet"*, it can sometimes present errors, so it is necessary to re-install to avoid future errors as you progress through the Floodlight environment.

After this, proceed to test that the *"Mininet"* has been correctly installed with the following command:

```
$ sudo mn
```

This command is used to enter the *"Mininet"* shell, where you can interact with the network topology and execute commands to configure and test different aspects of the emulated network.

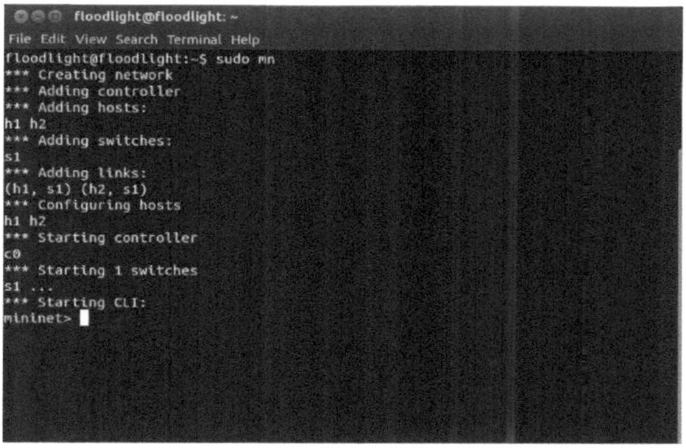

Figure 34. *Mininet execution*

After this, proceed to type the following command:

```
$ sudo mn --topo linear,3 --mac --controller=remote,ip=192.168.1.235,port=6653
--switch ovs,protocols=OpenFlow13
```

This command is used to start the emulation of a network using Mininet and connect it to a Floodlight controller on the designated port, which in this case is *"6653"*.

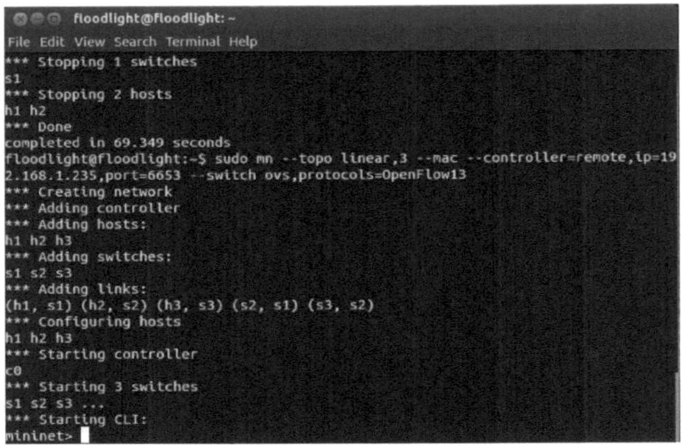

Figure 35. *Topology creation*

Once the command has been entered, it is verified that the topology has been created successfully. It should be noted that in the *"ip"* section, the IP of the network mask that corresponds to your machine must be entered.

Finally, type the following command:

```
$ pingall
```

This command is used within the Mininet environment to send a ping packet from each host to all other hosts in the virtual network topology.

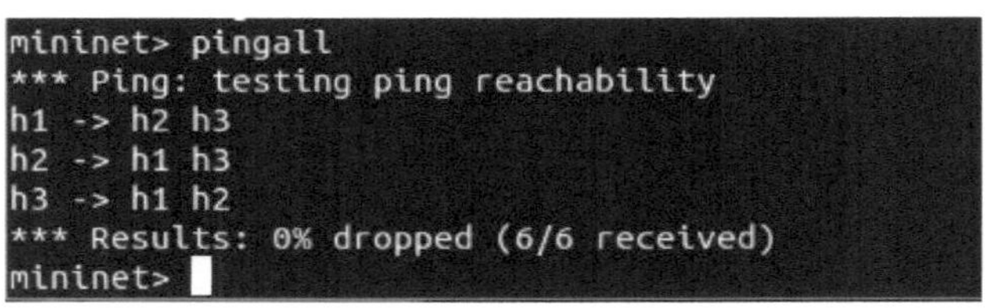

Figure 36. *Packet Test*

Once this is done, open the browser, for this it is necessary to go again to the *"Applications"* section.

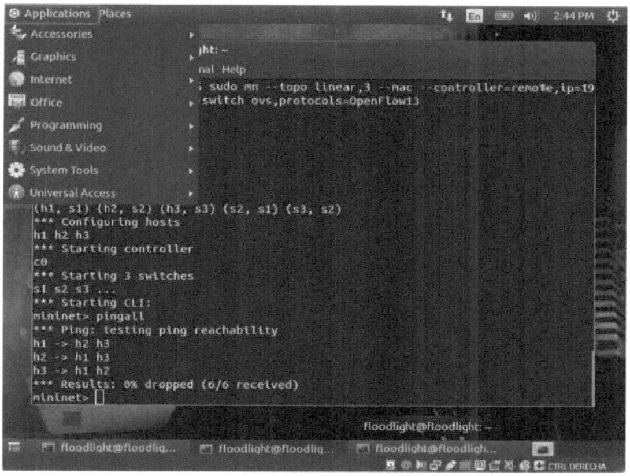

Figure 37. *Floodlight Virtual Machine (Applications) #2*

Once here, go to the *"Internet"* section and then to the browser.

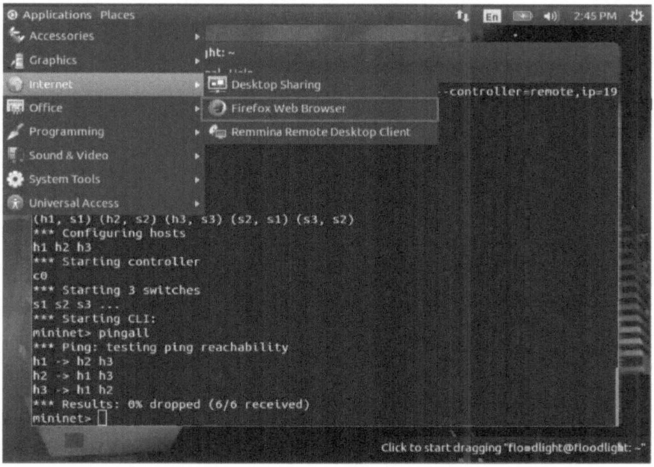

Figure 38. *Floodlight Options Box (Navigator)*

Once the browser is open, type the following link.

```
$ localhost:8080/ui/index.html
```

Once the link is entered, it should redirect you to the next section.

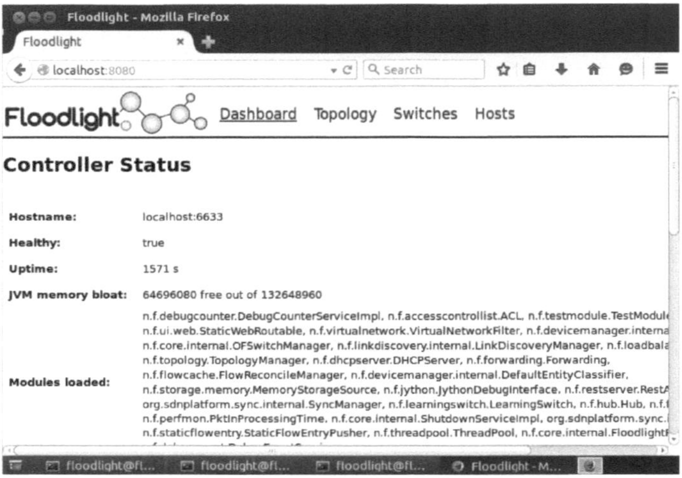

Figure 39. *Floodlight UI interface*

The link above refers to the Floodlight web administration panel home page.

When you run Floodlight and access this URL in your browser, you should be able to see the user interface (UI) of the Floodlight administration panel. From there, you can configure and manage the Floodlight controller, as well as view information about the OpenFlow network, topologies and flows.

It is important to note that this URL assumes that you have configured Floodlight to run on your local machine (localhost) and on port 8080. Make sure that the Floodlight driver is running and that you have correctly entered the URL in your browser to access the Floodlight user interface should an error occur.

The user interface of the Floodlight web administration panel. When you access this page, you will find various functionalities and sections that allow you to manage and configure the Floodlight controller. The following describes some of the common features you may find on this page:

- **Dashboard:** The initial control panel provides an overview of the network, including statistics, events and other relevant data.
- **Network Topology:** You can see a graphical representation of the network topology that Floodlight is managing. This includes the switches, links and connected hosts.
- **Switch management:** You can view and manage the OpenFlow switches connected to the Floodlight controller. This involves viewing their status, configuring them, modifying their rule flows and more.
- **Controller settings:** You can adjust Floodlight controller settings, such as the IP addresses and ports used, security settings and other specific options.
- **Monitoring and statistics:** You can obtain detailed information about network traffic, switch statistics, performance and other relevant data.
- **Rule flows:** You can examine and configure OpenFlow rule flows on Floodlight-managed switches. This includes viewing, editing and creating flows to control network behavior.

These are just some of the features you can find in the Floodlight user interface. The page provides a convenient way to manage and monitor the Floodlight controller and your network environment.

Now, previously, a linear topology of 3 hosts was created, Floodlight allows us to see this typology in a visual way, for this, from the User Interface of the controller we access the section called *"Topology"*.

Figure 40. *Floodlight UI interface #2*

Once clicked, it immediately redirects us to the topology section and we will find the topology that was previously created.

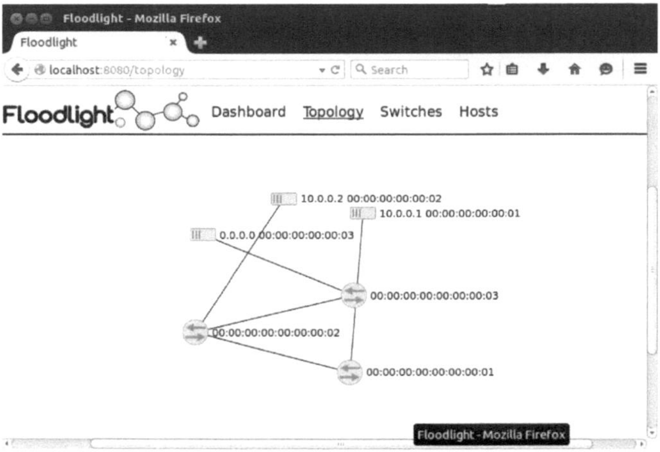

Figure 41. *Floodlight UI interface - Topology*

As we can see, the topology that was created by us is perfectly displayed. In addition to this it is also possible to ping between them and test the connectivity between the hosts of the emulated network with the following command.

```
$ h1 ping h2
```

```
mininet> h1 ping h2
PING 10.0.0.2 (10.0.0.2) 56(84) bytes of data.
64 bytes from 10.0.0.2: icmp_seq=1 ttl=64 time=2.99 ms
64 bytes from 10.0.0.2: icmp_seq=2 ttl=64 time=0.143 ms
64 bytes from 10.0.0.2: icmp_seq=3 ttl=64 time=0.033 ms
64 bytes from 10.0.0.2: icmp_seq=4 ttl=64 time=0.036 ms
64 bytes from 10.0.0.2: icmp_seq=5 ttl=64 time=0.038 ms
64 bytes from 10.0.0.2: icmp_seq=6 ttl=64 time=0.025 ms
64 bytes from 10.0.0.2: icmp_seq=7 ttl=64 time=0.039 ms
```

Figure 42. *Packet Test #2*

As we can see the connectivity between the hosts of the network is done correctly. In order to finish testing the connectivity we do the following shortcut in the system.

```
$ ctrl + c
```

This will immediately cancel the connectivity test, now type the following command to

```
$ exit
```

exit *"Mininet"*.

After this, if you go back to the *"Topology"* section, it will show the following:

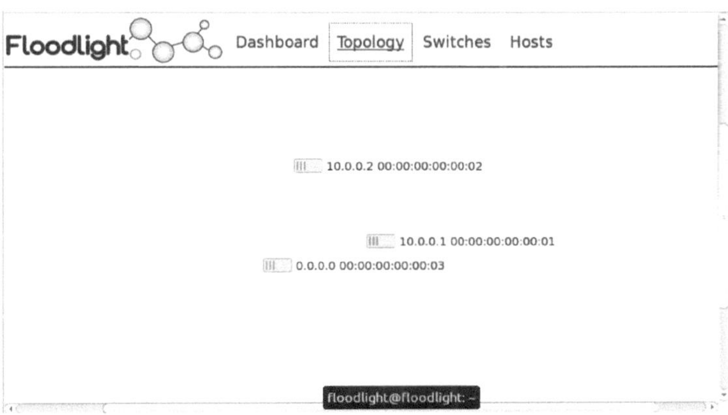

Figure 43. *Floodlight UI interface - Topology #2*

As could be observed, when leaving the *"Mininet"* section, the topology previously created disappeared, which means that it stopped receiving the connection it had.

Now we will try to make a test with a different topology, for this it is necessary to type the following command.

```
$ sudo mn --controller=remote, ip=192.168.1.235,port=6653 --switch ovsk,
protocols=OpenFlow13
```

Once the command has been typed, we can see the following topology in the *"Topology"* section

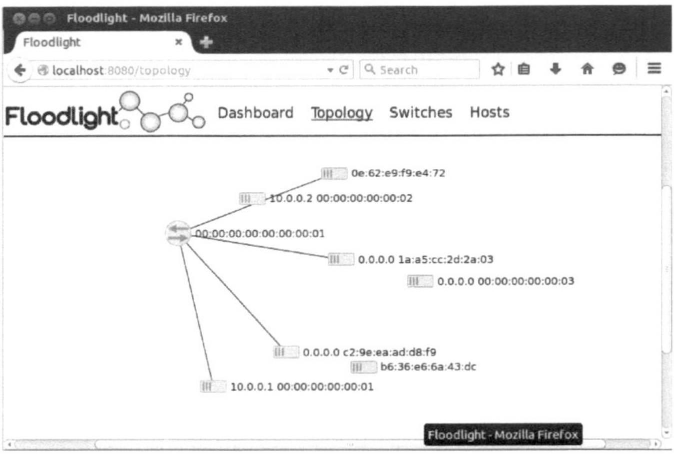

Figure 44. *Floodlight UI Interface - Topology #3*

This new topology unlike the previous one does not specify a specific network topology, so it starts a basic topology with a single switch and two hosts, we can also try to do a connectivity test.

```
$ h1 ping h2
```

```
mininet> h1 ping h2
PING 10.0.0.2 (10.0.0.2) 56(84) bytes of data.
64 bytes from 10.0.0.2: icmp_seq=1 ttl=64 time=1.39 ms
64 bytes from 10.0.0.2: icmp_seq=2 ttl=64 time=0.111 ms
64 bytes from 10.0.0.2: icmp_seq=3 ttl=64 time=0.026 ms
64 bytes from 10.0.0.2: icmp_seq=4 ttl=64 time=0.030 ms
```

Figure 45. *Packet Test #3*

As we can see, the connectivity is also performed correctly, and it is even able to be done in reverse, with the command.

```
$ h2 ping h1
```

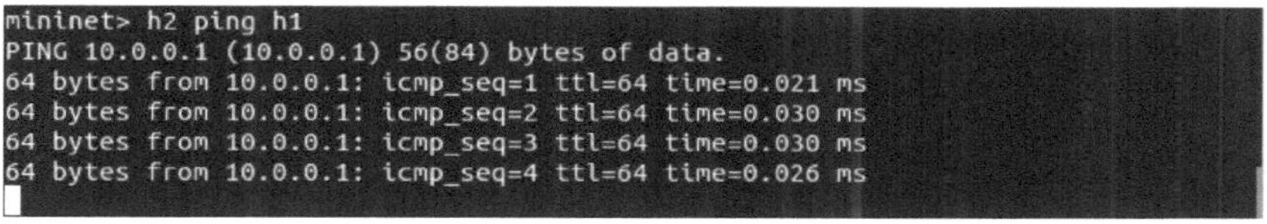

Figure 46. *Packet Test #4*

Now host *"h2"* sends ping packets to host *"h1"* and it shows a successful response.

CHAPTER 5

USING FLOODLIGHT

Now that the Floodlight environment has been well executed, it is possible to make use of the capabilities that this framework can provide to the user. For example, when creating topologies, it was previously observed how, when creating them, these could be observed in the user interface that Floodlight provided, exactly the same thing will be done, but with different types of topologies, which will be observed and then the results will be shown in the interface.

Previously a basic topology was tested where the network was simple, with three hosts

```
$ sudo mn --topo linear,4 --mac --controller=remote,ip=192.168.1.235,port=6653
--switch ovs,protocols=OpenFlow13
```

and a switch, but this can be extended, for example.

This command will expand the range of the topology from 3 to 4, which may show something similar to what you can see below.

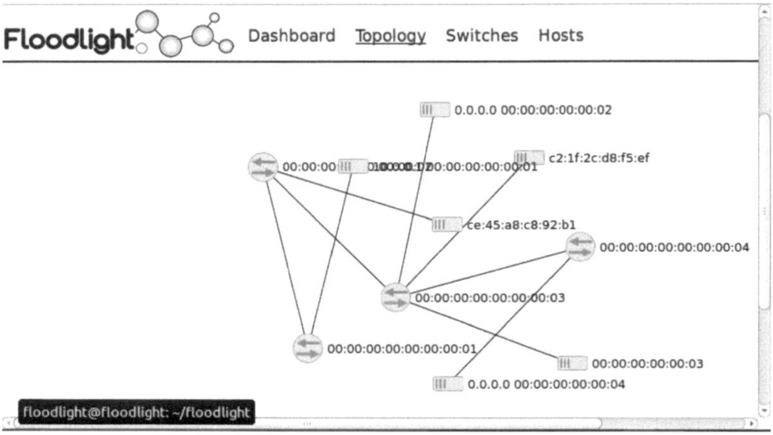

Figure 47. *Floodlight UI Interface - Topology #3*

As can be seen in this topology, there is a central switch and three hosts connected to it, unlike the previous one where there were three hosts and one switch, which was not centralized.

Now, again an increment will be made to observe what can happen with the topology, for this it will be required to raise once more the value of the topology in the command

```
$ sudo mn --topo linear,5 --mac --controller=remote,ip=192.168.1.235,port=6653
--switch ovs,protocols=OpenFlow13
```

as shown below.

After typing the command, you will go to the Floodlight environment once again and in the topology section you will see the following:

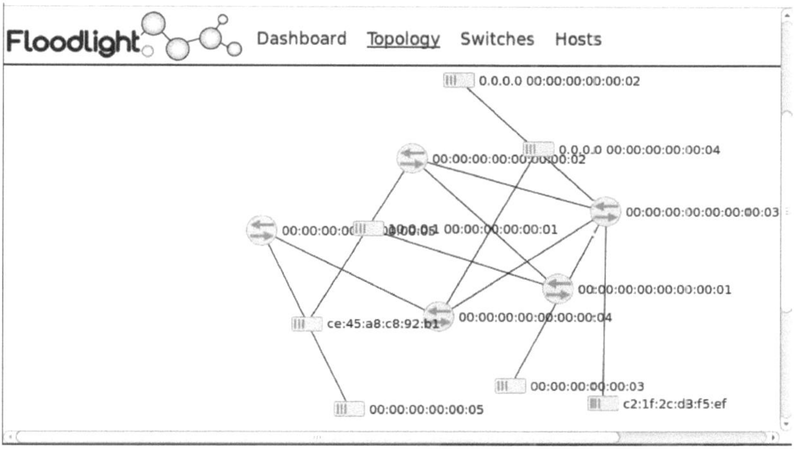

Figure 48. *Floodlight UI interface - Topology #4*

In this topology, we proceed to increase the value from 4 to 5, and we can see that we have five switches and four hosts, where each host is connected to a different switch.

It is also possible to create and visualize tree topologies by typing the following command.

```
sudo mn -topo tree, depth=2,fanout=2 -mac -controller=remote,ip=192.168.1.235,port=6653
-switch ovs,protocols=OpenFlow13
```

After typing the command, you will again go to the Floodlight environment in the topology section and you will see the following:

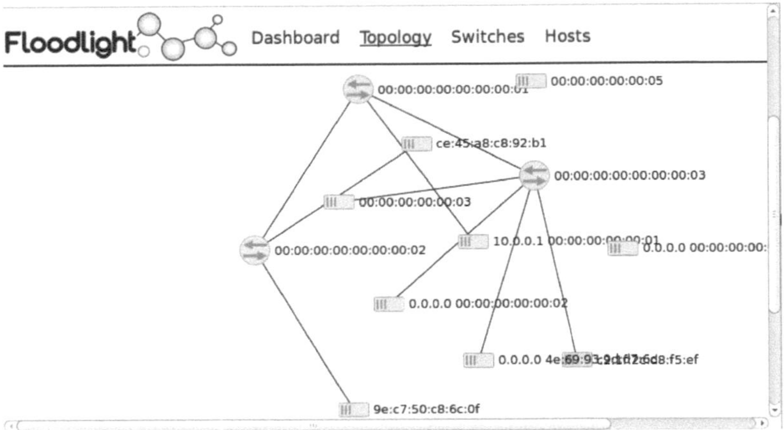

Figure 49. *Floodlight UI interface - Topology #5*

Here you can see the previously created topology, which consists of a root switch and four secondary switches, each with one host connected.

We have already seen how linear and tree topologies can be created, but it is also possible to create custom topologies, and for this it is necessary to take into account that to create it it is necessary to have a Python file with the topology specifications. For example.

We have the following code.

```
from mininet.topo import Topo

class MyTopology(Topo):
    def __init__(self):
        Topo.__init__(self)

        # Add switches
        switch1 = self.addSwitch('s1')
        switch2 = self.addSwitch('s2')

        # Add hosts
        host1 = self.addHost('h1')
        host2 = self.addHost('h2')

        # Connecting switches and hosts
        self.addLink(host1, switch1)
        self.addLink(host2, switch2)
        self.addLink(switch1, switch2)

topos = {'mytopo': (lambda: MyTopology())}
```

In this code it can be seen that a basic topology is being created as the ones seen previously and this can be evidenced by the small number of switches and hosts that this code has. Once the code is written, it will have to be saved as a *".py"* file, this is because it is a Python code since Mininet only accepts the Python language.

The name that will be placed to the file can be any as long as it ends in *".py"*, after this it will be saved in the Floodlight folder, which can be found in the following section.

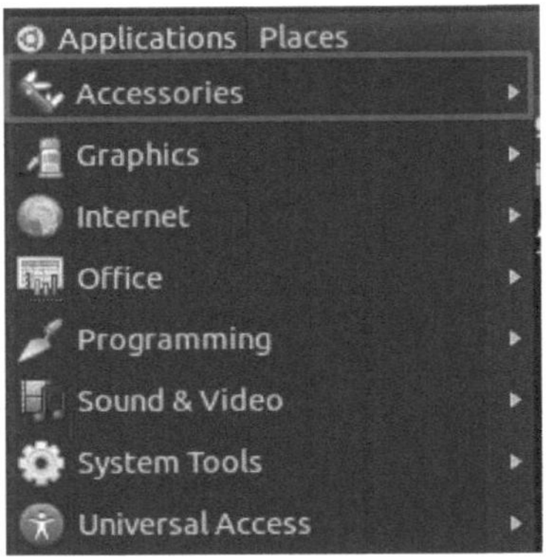

Figure 50. *Applications - Floodlight*

After entering *"Accessories"*, go to the *"Files"* section.

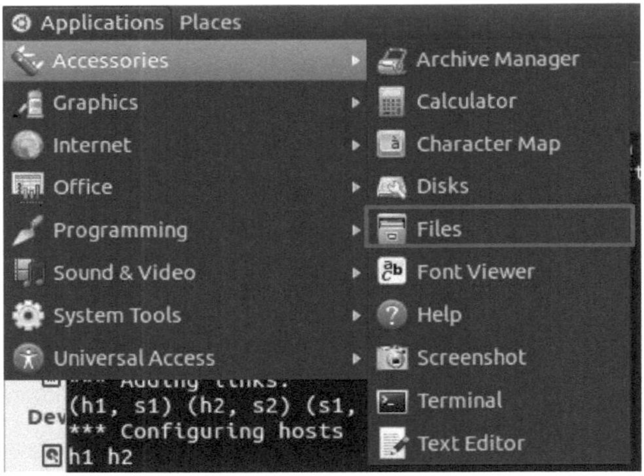

Figure 51. *Floodlight Options Box (Files)*

Once we click on the *"Files"* section, a window like the one shown below will open.

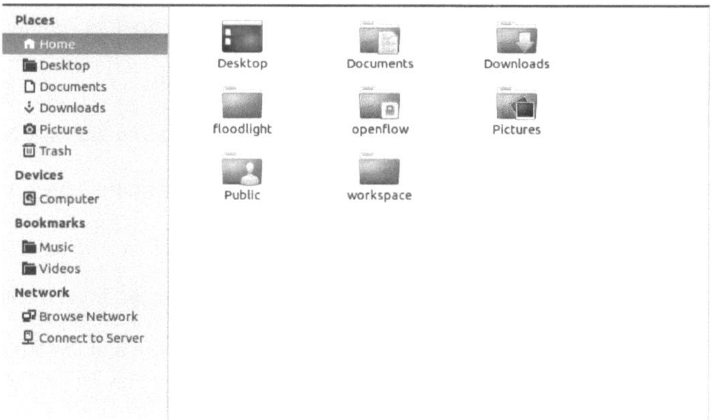

Figure 52. *Task Manager - Floodlight*

In this section you can find the Floodlight folder where the file will be saved to be executed later, in this case the file is called *"mytopo.py"* and in the terminal the following command will be typed:

```
sudo mn --custom mytopo.py --topo mytopo --mac --controller=remote,
ip=192.168.1.235,port=6653 --switch ovs,protocols=OpenFlow13
```

This command loads the topology defined in the created file *"mytopo.py"* and uses it to create the network in Mininet, as a result you will get the following:

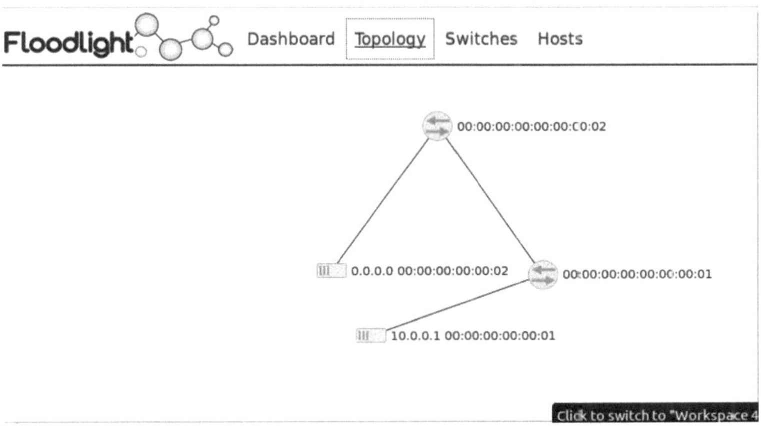

Figure 53. *Floodlight UI Interface - Topology #6*

This will have created a customized topology where each host is connected to its switch according to the configuration made in the Python code.

It is also possible to customize the links, for this the following exercise will be done.

- A topology will be created with four switches and five hosts where some links have limited bandwidth and others have added latency.

For this it will be necessary to create a topology with customized links in Mininet, the *"-link"* command will be used to specify some of the characteristics of the links between

```
sudo mn --topo linear,4 --link tc,bw=10 --link tc,delay=5ms --link tc,bw=20 --link
tc,delay=10ms
```

the nodes. This will be done by typing the following command.

After typing the command, you will again go to the Floodlight environment in the topology section and you will see the following:

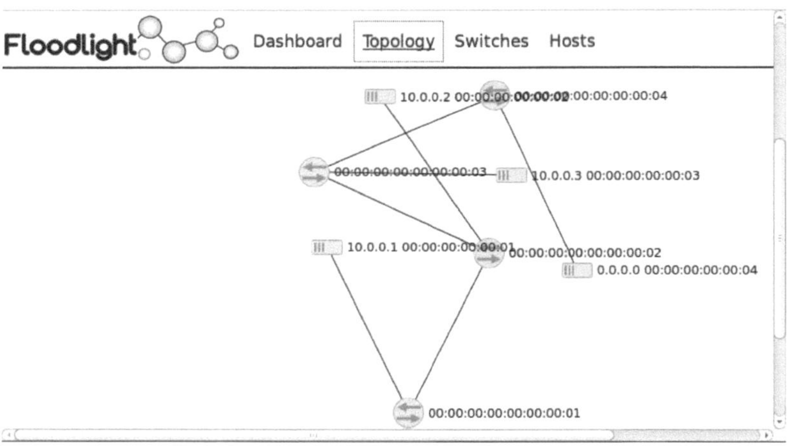

Figure 54. *Floodlight UI Interface - Topology #7*

You can check if it worked by doing a packet test and this can be done between the different hosts you have, as you can see below.

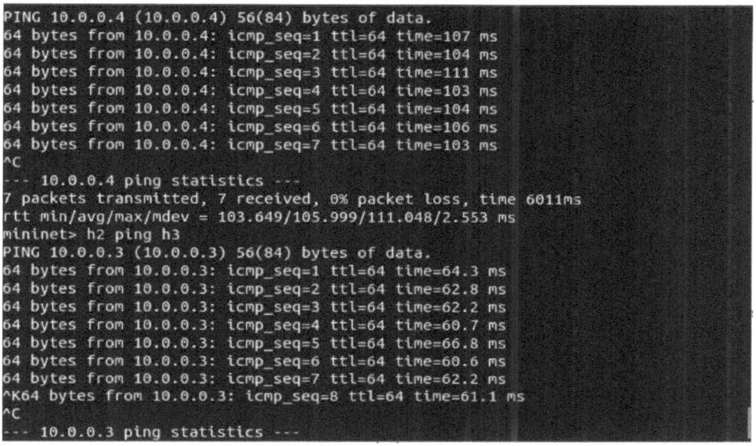

Figure 55. *Packet Test #5*

This concludes the entire journey of using the Floodlight controller. Throughout this journey, the fascinating world of Software Defined Networking (SDN) and its implementation using the Floodlight controller has been explored in depth. It has also been possible to see how SDN represents a paradigm shift in network management and architecture, offering greater flexibility, scalability and centralized control.

The Floodlight controller, as an open source platform, provides a practical window into this revolutionary approach. By installing and configuring it in a virtual environment, it has been possible to experience first-hand the capabilities of SDN and its potential to simplify and optimize network management.

Virtual machines have played a crucial role in this process by providing an isolated and flexible environment to experiment and develop SDN solutions without putting the existing network infrastructure at risk. The synergy between SDN and virtualization has proven to be a powerful combination for driving innovation and agility in the networking world.

As we move towards an increasingly connected and network-dependent future, SDN and tools such as Floodlight are positioned as cornerstones to address the challenges and take advantage of the opportunities that lie ahead. The ability to centrally schedule and control network behavior will enable organizations to quickly adapt to changing requirements and demands, thereby optimizing the performance and efficiency of their network infrastructures.

References

Shaghaghi, A., Kaafar, M. A., Buyya, R., & Jha, S. (2020). Software-defined network (SDN) data plane security: issues, solutions, and future directions. Handbook of Computer Networks and Cyber Security: Principles and Paradigms, 341-387.

Jiang, X., Xu, X., Zhang, J., Shen, F., Cao, Z., & Shen, H. T. (2022). Sdn: Semantic decoupling network for temporal language grounding. IEEE Transactions on Neural Networks and Learning Systems.

Alotaibi, H. S., Gregory, M. A., & Li, S. (2022). Multidomain sdn-based gateways and border gateway protocol. Journal of Computer Networks and Communications, 2022.

Jimenez, M. B., Fernandez, D., Rivadeneira, J. E., Bellido, L., & Cardenas, A. (2021). A survey of the main security issues and solutions for the SDN architecture. IEEE Access, 9, 122016-122038.

Wazirali, R., Ahmad, R., & Alhiyari, S. (2021). SDN-openflow topology discovery: an overview of performance issues. Applied Sciences, 11(15), 6999.

Pei, J., Hong, P., Xue, K., Li, D., Wei, D. S., & Wu, F. (2020). Two-phase virtual network function selection and chaining algorithm based on deep learning in SDN/NFV-enabled networks. IEEE Journal on Selected Areas in Communications, 38(6), 1102-1117.

Das, T., & Gurusamy, M. (2021). Multi-objective control plane dimensioning in hybrid SDN/legacy networks. IEEE Transactions on Network and Service Management, 18(3), 2929-2942.

Wazirali, R., Ahmad, R., & Alhiyari, S. (2021). SDN-openflow topology discovery: an overview of performance issues. Applied Sciences, 11(15), 6999.

Dias, A. H., Correia, L. H., & Malheiros, N. (2021). A systematic literature review on virtual machine consolidation. ACM Computing Surveys (CSUR), 54(8), 1-38.Dias, A. H., Correia, L. H., & Malheiros, N. (2021). A systematic literature review on virtual machine consolidation. ACM Computing Surveys (CSUR), 54(8), 1-38.

Yang, Z., & Yeung, K. L. (2020). Flow monitoring scheme design in SDN. Computer Networks, 167, 107007.

Yoo, Y., Yang, G., Lee, J., Shin, C., Kim, H., & Yoo, C. (2022). TeaVisor: network hypervisor for bandwidth isolation in SDN-NV. IEEE Transactions on Cloud Computing.

Aryan, R., Yazidi, A., Brattensborg, F., Kure, Ø., & Engelstad, P. E. (2022). SDN Spotlight: A real-time OpenFlow troubleshooting framework. Future Generation Computer Systems, 133, 364-377.

Qu, K., Zhuang, W., Ye, Q., Shen, X., Li, X., & Rao, J. (2020). Dynamic flow migration for embedded services in SDN/NFV-enabled 5G core networks. IEEE Transactions on Communications, 68(4), 2394-2408.

Umar, R., Riadi, I., & Kusuma, R. S. (2021). Mitigating sodinokibi ransomware attack on cloud network using software-defined networking (SDN). International Journal of Safety and Security Engineering, 11(3), 239-246.

Hamdan, M., Hassan, E., Abdelaziz, A., Elhigazi, A., Mohammed, B., Khan, S., ... & Marsono, M. N. (2021). A comprehensive survey of load balancing techniques in software-defined network. Journal of Network and Computer Applications, 174, 102856.

Links.

https://github.com/floodlight/floodlight

https://www.researchgate.net/figure/Internal-architecture-of-the-Floodlight-controller-and-its-interfaces_fig12_319385426

https://www.researchgate.net/figure/Floodlight-SDN-controller-architecture-Further-f-Forwarding-It-is-forwarding_fig1_323057223

https://www.sdxcentral.com/networking/sdn/definitions/what-the-definition-of-software-defined-networking-sdn/what-is-sdn-controller/openflow-controller/what-is-floodlight-controller/

https://www.telefonicaempresas.es/grandes-empresas/blog/sdn-en-las-redes-el-origen-de-una-transformacion/

https://dialnet.unirioja.es/descarga/articulo/4897871.pdf

https://alb3rtoalonso.com/2021/03/18/sdn-nfv-openflow-innovacion-en-las-redes/

https://www.computerweekly.com/es/definicion/OpenFlow

https://opennetworking.org/mininet/

https://www.sdxcentral.com/networking/sdn/definitions/what-the-definition-of-software-defined-networking-sdn/what-is-sdn-controller/openflow-controller/what-is-floodlight-controller/

https://floodlight.atlassian.net/wiki/spaces/floodlightcontroller/pages/1343544/Installation+Guide#InstallationGuide-Installation

MIX
Papier aus verantwortungsvollen Quellen
Paper from responsible sources
FSC® C105338

Printed by Books on Demand GmbH, Norderstedt / Germany